A Writer's Guide to the Zodiac

How the stars can help you understand your characters

Giselle Green

AMHERST

This one is for Eliott

**For further copies of this book, or for a consultation,
the author may be contacted via email on gisellesgreen@aol.com,
or by telephone on 01634 868809.**

ISBN 1 903637 31 7

Printed in Great Britain

First published in 2005 by

Amherst Publishing Limited
Longmore House, High Street, Otford, Sevenoaks, Kent TN14 5PQ

Contents

Everything begins with energy

People are like colours; and, like colours, their personalities come in every conceivable shade and variety and hue. But imagine an artist who has only reds and browns available on his palette. He will be more inclined to paint autumnal scenes or fields of poppies than he will seascapes. In other words, particular colours lend themselves to certain types of picture. In just the same way, people who have a particular type of energy will tend towards a certain type of personality.

And, just as there are only three primary colours – Red, Yellow and Blue, which all the others derive from, we can think of peoples' personalities as having a basis in just four primary types of energy. These correspond to the elements of Earth, Air, Fire and Water.

When creating characters it is a useful point to remember that *people will do what it is in their nature to do.* And a character's nature can be very usefully described in terms of which of these four types of energy he gravitates most towards.

What this book aims to do is give you some insight into what drives characters *from the inside.* Whilst there may be dozens of ways that a writer can build up a character profile, if a character isn't 'working' it could well be because he/she has been built up rather like a cardboard cut-out dolly, the sort little girls used to 'dress up' with different cut-out clothes. You can dress the dolly according to whatever your mood dictates (e.g. your character notes may run along the lines of; green eyes, brown hair, likes cheese, grows daffodils in pots in the spring…) but if you want to create a living, breathing, self-directing character, you'll need to go one further than that.

If you start by having an understanding of your character's energy then you'll have a line into their pulse, into their heartbeat. You'll have an intuitive sense of what are their most pressing needs, their deepest motivations.

To return to the colour analogy for a moment, if you see

someone dressed from head to toe in red, you aren't going to expect them to be a shy and retiring sort. Someone dressed entirely in blue will give off a more serene, maybe sober air, and a very yellowy-attired person will suggest someone young, creative and sunny in disposition. The same kind of thinking can be applied with respect to the four energies that go into making up personalities; this is what we will look at next.

The colours of the Zodiac;
Earth, Air, Fire and Water

(And what if you don't believe in Astrology?)

The good news is that you don't have to believe in, or know anything about astrology, in order for this system to work. There is no need for you to know anything about the stars. You just need to want to get to know your characters better.

And it is easy enough. Just for the moment, accept the premise that the make-up of individuals can be expressed as a combination of each of the four different types of energy - Earth, Air, Fire and Water. Accept that each of these elements expresses a certain *way of being* in the world.

You will already have a pretty good idea what I mean by this term 'a way of being' because we use 'elemental' language every day when we want to describe people. For instance we'll say that someone has a 'fiery' or 'combustible' nature (fire) or we'll describe them as being a 'wet blanket' or just 'wet' (water) or we can say that they're 'airy fairy' or 'in their heads' (air) or that they're the 'salt of the earth' or 'well-grounded' or plain 'earthy' (earth).

Another way to think about these different elements is that they are like different radio stations that people might tune into. On one wavelength you may find primarily classical music. It's easy enough to imagine that people who are drawn to this will on the whole conform to a particular character profile. We might expect to find this audience a quieter bunch, more reflective, maybe they find their nerves more easily jarred than those who listen to the heavy metal station. The head-bangers will on the whole be more outgoing and will need peace less than they need stimulation. Why is it that some people prefer to spend their Sundays jumping out of planes on parachutes while others would rather be pottering round garden centres?

Knowing what your character really wants

The problem for writers who are working on characters just using their instinct alone, becomes that instinct can be a moody beast. It isn't always reliable. You can *think* you know a character (from his aunt's maiden name right down to the colour of his boxer shorts) and then – hey presto – he goes and does something unexpected and uncalled for and really rather *out of character*. And, what is worse, something not conducive to the plot.

You need to get them back in line (or better still, make sure you keep them in line in the first place). One way to do this is to have a really good understanding of what the four above-mentioned elements mean in terms of the human psyche.

Is a 'fire' person really only going to be 'fiery' in nature? Is a water person always going to be either 'refreshing' or a 'wet blanket'? Not always. But there are certain fundamental things that people who belong to each of the elemental groups *will* have in common. You can think of this as an orientation of character.

Some people, for instance, are ultra-sensitive to psychic phenomena and things like ghosts, whereas other folk, who might scoff at the idea of ghosts, are extremely sensitive to matters of importance to *them* such as their social status. Maybe this faction wouldn't dream of inviting any friends around to see a new home without having the whole place redecorated first. The former group mightn't be so worried about the wallpaper but might make sure that they'd conducted something like a 'house-cleansing' ritual before moving in or having anyone round. The two groups are clearly oriented towards different things; the matters that feel 'real' to them in their lives are very different things. We say that they are 'coming from' a different place. What we mean is that they are more in touch with one element than they are another. What you are in touch with is what is real to you.

This is the kind of thing you can pick up by looking at a person's elemental balance. Some folk will be mostly in touch with the realm of feelings. These are the water people. Others will be in touch with something else. Air people will be in touch with their thoughts. Fire people will be in touch with their dreams, their imagination. Earth people will best understand the mundane world of the everyday.

By knowing what element a character is most in touch with, you can find out what it is that matters most to them. When you know that you will know what their motivation is. So when you get a slippery character who tries to sneak off and do something not in your plan you can let them do it as long as you bear in mind what it is that they *really* want, in their deepest heart of hearts.

According to the astrological system there are twelve things that people might really want, and these are given by the meanings of the zodiac signs.

Now let us turn to the zodiac.

How do we get the twelve signs from just four elements?

If you're wondering how we get twelve zodiac signs from just four elements, its simple; there are three types of each, three 'Fires', three 'Earths', three 'Waters' and three 'Airs'.

Why *three,* you might ask? Well, it's the same as when we're writing a book; we need 'A beginning, a middle and an end'. If you think about it, having a 'beginning, a middle and an end' is something intrinsic to *any* process you can imagine. In astrology, we refer to these stages as 'cardinal', 'fixed', and 'mutable'.

The three signs which correspond to each of the elements do just this; for instance, the first Water sign (Cancer) serves to 'open up' or *begin* the element of water, in other words it starts the action. Scorpio is in the middle so it keeps the water action going and then Pisces the last water element ends it and allows the energy to change to something else.

How might this be expressed in terms of personality? Well, Cancerians are said to be quite willing to take the initiative (they 'open up the action', set the ball rolling, start the story off), Scorpios are often said to be very persevering and set in their ways (they are in the middle so their role is to 'keep things going as they are', neither initiating or ending things), and Pisceans are described more often than not as being 'emotional, indecisive and changeable' (sorry, Pisceans!) – because their whole purpose is directed towards *changing* the status quo and moving onto something else (i.e. they represent the 'end').

And what exactly is it that these characters are driven to 'take the initiative', 'keep as they are', or 'change the status quo' on? They are driven to do these things *with respect to the element which they represent.* In the example just given, the element (type of energy) which they represent is Water. So let's start by looking a little closer at each of these elements and discovering how they are expressed at the level of the personality and the human psyche.

PART ONE

WATER

The WATER element – the element of feelings and emotional connectedness

In astrology the water element represents the realm of deep emotions and intuitive feelings. It represents the ability to pick up on nuances and atmospheres. Water is a 'Yin' element, representing the feminine domain (in both males and females). Writers of women's fiction in particular tend to be strong in this element because expressing emotions and feelings is obviously easier for people who are already clued into water.

Let us think for a minute what is the true nature of water. What is it *like?*

How does it appear to us in nature; what can it do? Stop for a minute and realise that if you *really tune in* to this element you will gain a perfect understanding of what water people are like. Imagine a light shower of rain gently pattering down into a parched garden on a hot summer's day.

The parched garden can be likened to someone who is feeling emotionally arid; they are feeling like a dried up husk, emotionless, in a place where nothing can touch them. Somebody going through bereavement might go through a stage of feeling just like this, or someone who has been through a lot of trauma. The relief provided by the gentle rain is like the relief felt when a person begins to 'feel' again after a long period of feeling 'dried up' and out of touch. Like the earth, a person who remains out of touch with their feelings for too long may feel that they are beginning to 'crack up'.

The function of the water element within the personality is a cohesive one; our emotions and feelings are what 'hold us together'. Now imagine that the rain starts falling harder; it becomes a torrent. The riverbed swells and overflows. The land begins to get flooded. The formerly arid land has become drenched and water-logged. Astrologically-speaking, anyone over-saturated with the water element is likely to start feeling very 'heavy' and 'down' and feel as if they are 'sinking' – all familiar feelings to anyone who suffers from occasional depression. Whilst we might describe someone who puts us back in touch with our feelings as 'refreshing' (think small, cute person who reminds us what the really important stuff in life is all about), a character like 'Eeyore' from Winnie the Pooh is definitely suffering from an overdose of the water element. So was Miss Haversham in Dickens' 'Great Expectations'.

Talking of Miss Haversham, this is a good point to mention that **the time frame which the water element relates to is the Past**. Watery people are often nostalgic and clingy and like to reminisce about 'how things were' (and this is regardless of whether or not the past was particularly good or bad; it is just the place where they prefer to dwell). Decrepit old Miss Haversham was so far stuck in the past as to believe herself still to be a blushing young bride. But part of her knew that she wasn't. Part of her still wanted revenge on men – all men, or any man – for her mistreatment, which is why she sets up our unsuspecting hero Pip with Estella who has been trained to be as emotionally manipulative as her mistress.

Water cleanses us, outside and in, and the water element – in its 'good' guise is designed to have exactly that effect on the human psyche. We can all appreciate the cathartic effects of having a good cry at times. That's why we love to watch 'weepies'; we feel like we've had a good 'spring cleaning' afterwards. We feel lighter and fresher and less clogged up. Just like we feel better after having a shower even when we didn't feel particularly dirty in the first place!

But note – if we are already very watery people (emotional, empathic and sentimental), who can be moved to tears at the slightest thing – then we probably don't want to watch weepies. It would be akin to someone standing in the shower for far too long... they'd end up wrinkly and soggy!

Water acts as a channel – very watery people can be mediumistic

In nature, one of the most important functions of water is its ability to transport things around. It can do this either by dissolving them first or just simply by using the sheer force and weight of its own volume to push things along. In terms of how water acts in the psyche, we can think of water as being a conduit – a means of passage, or a channel – for other energies.

People with very 'watery' astrological charts are highly intuitive, sensitive and psychically tuned-in, whether they are aware of this or not. One consequence of this finely-tuned ability to pick up on every little nuance and sensitivity to atmospheres is that watery people really do need to spend time on their own to 'chill out' and get away from other people's energies which are felt so keenly as to be rather intrusive.

The more sensitive (i.e. watery) the person, the more they might experience the periodic need for withdrawal. Yet before you run away with the idea that water people are best suited as hermits, to live far away from the rest of the human race, the opposite is in fact true. Watery people must be allowed their space and at the same time be encouraged to interact and connect with other people wherever possible. This is because their sensitivity makes them the most compassionate and giving of people; they make excellent care-givers because their capacity for empathy is so high. Remember that it is a *primary function of water to act as a conduit for other energies.*

What might characters that are primarily tuned into the water element be like then?

They will be just like water itself is. They will be channels for emotional communication between people. Just as water always tries to find its own level, Water people will easily tune in to 'emotions' and 'feelings' floating around in the atmosphere, the invisible 'ambiance' that gives a place its flavour and character even though none of it will be visible to the eye. Basically, their emotional nature will seek to 'join up' with the emotional strains of what has gone before, just as bodies of water will always join and merge together given half a chance. They are not just sympathetic, they are empathic, other people's feelings will be as their own. They can put themselves, emotionally *in exactly the same place* as the other person who is going through the strong feelings. They can become as one with them. Water molecules merge into a body of water completely and absolutely. They don't maintain their boundaries. Sometimes water people don't maintain good boundaries either. They may ask questions that other people would not dare to ask. They may seep into your life or right under your skin till you feel they have got into a place they have no right to be.

And they can be touchy! As feelings are subjective, everything is taken so *personally,* even when it isn't intended as such.

They will be in touch with the past, and have a love of history and antiques and places of historical interest. They will research genealogies, sinking down into the roots of ancestral lines as easily as rainwater permeates the soil, feeding the roots of the vegetation that grows upon it.

Remember that a conduit is just that – a channel. When the channel is blocked for some reason, the answer is to relax and stop trying. Concentrating too hard is like trying to suck juice up through a straw which your fingers are clasping too tightly and constricting in the middle. Watery people really need to learn to 'go with the flow' and just channel in whatever is coming in on the tide. I know several writers who write like this – particularly when they're writing very fast and it all just streams out. They have reported that, when they have needed to re-write some pages later on (if they had lost some pages in the middle, for example), and then subsequently found the original pages, that the two passages read almost word for word the same.

In fiction, we might expect water characters to be the ones who invariably prod or provoke the other characters into outpourings or expressions of emotion, if indeed they aren't doing it themselves. To put it another way, as far as water is concerned water wants to be moving, one way or another. If stuck for knowing how a character will behave in a certain situation, think of how the elements appear in nature. If a water character encounters a Fire character, water plus heat equals steam (could be a sensuous encounter, or just the two of them letting off steam?), or it could mean a dowsing of the fire, in which case we see one person's ardour being 'cooled off', their passion quenched by the water.

It is in the nature of water to soak into the earth, interpenetrating with the particles of soil and seeping right through it; basically, an emotional character may provoke movement in a stuck or clogged up earthy, more pragmatic character.

Now imagine a character who has become like water left in a standing pool, stagnant and heavy. They become the wet blankets, the 'party poopers' unwilling to take risks or for anyone else to do so, either. Like a water-logged field, they inhibit the movement and growth of all around them. Taking the water-logging analogy a bit further, the character may become depressed and sink into a chasm of unmoving feeling-energy, desperate to get out and yet feeling far too heavy to do so.

But remember, land-locked water which has no conduit to flow through can always escape through evaporation. In such a case, air and fire prove to be water's allies. In other words, your character can talk over their troubles (air equals communication) with another character, or can find someone to remind them what they have yet to do, bring their future back into focus by capturing their imagination (which is the function of fire).

What this really means for water people is that it is in their nature to constantly let their feelings 'take them on a journey' (be it seeping through the earth down into the bedrock or soaring up to the clouds as evaporation).

If a watery person meets an 'airy' personality, they may be moved to 'make waves' or else the feelings needing to be expressed may 'evaporate' in that locality (or fictional scene) only to reappear in the same way that water does, re-condensing elsewhere later on. An intellectual boss, for example, may speak coldly and unfeelingly to a sensitive secretary who, unable to do anything else, relocates her distress until a later scene where she is able to cry about it.

A watery personality meeting an 'earth' personality will probably feel quite relieved. Earth contains and harbours water; it provides a safe vessel for it, a 'place to be' (which is all good as long as the earth is like the channel of a river bed and allows that water to flow). And of course, the characteristic of water whereby it takes on the shape of whatever it is contained in, harks back to the *empathy* of the water people. They can take on other people's emotions all too easily at times. Now let us look at the three types of characters that represent the element of water.

Cancer - for nurturing, nostalgic, mothering and good-at-listening characters

Cancerians are the ones who 'open up the action' with the element of water. At first sight this may seem strange. Most people understand Cancer to be one of the most cautious and conservative of signs – which it is – and not always one which will readily take the initiative in things. Crabs move side wards, and Cancerians are likewise said to go for a lateral line of attack on whatever they fancy.

Nonetheless, if the thing being 'opened up' has anything to do with the emotional realm, then Cancerians will be the ones to do it. This is why Cancerians often make such good counsellors and therapists; they make good listeners, who hear and respond with the heart.

In fiction, they will often be cast in the role of the wise friend who offers the shoulder to cry on, the character with the emotional wisdom to see what is really happening. If they are the main character, they will be motivated by the strong desire to forge human relationships, emotional connections, and create families. No role in life expresses all the above more perfectly than that of Mother. And Cancer, of course, is ruled by the Moon, the planet which represents 'mother' in the chart.

Meggie Cleary (from Colleen Mc McCullough's 'TheThorn Birds') is one such character. When Meggie's own mother rejects her baby son Hal, we are told that little Meggie steps in seamlessly to become his surrogate mother. From the beginning we are aware that all Meggie ever really wants, is someone of her own to love. For Meggie, emotion flows easily and naturally, unlike for her mother Fee who appears to be as cold as stone. When her beloved priest Ralph comes to see her after baby Hal tragically dies, Ralph is bowled over by her smile at him, which is described as overflowing with love, despite her pain.

Whereas, contrast Meggie's way of being with her mother's.

Fee doesn't cry and no one even knows whether Fee is grieving. Fee too, feels things so intensely that the only way she can cope is to shut everything down entirely. Yet her life is full of incredible pain, almost as if some invisible force were trying its hardest to get her to admit to what she so totally denies – her human feelings.

The concept of 'mother' is a good one to keep in mind if you want to get a really good handle on your Cancerian characters. No matter what form a personal 'mother' takes, any character who is primarily nurturing in temperament will have to walk a fine line to make sure that they do not become 'smothering' and over-involved. A friend who starts off giving out well-meant and well-received advice might well not know when its time to back off …and end up being more interfering than helpful. Characters who are nurturing and giving by nature are wonderful to have around when you need to receive; when it's time to move on and metaphorically 'fly the nest', then the 'nurturer' needs to have a new clutch of eggs to brood over or she's going to pursue you!

A Cancerian character will initiate the flow of emotion between themselves and others or facilitate the passage of feelings between others.

They might also sometimes be experienced as people who 'rock the boat' – or upset things just when it seems that everyone is getting along just fine. The truth is, that if people *really* are getting along fine, it will not be so easy for anyone to rock the boat. The Cancerian will pick up the emotional undercurrents of disharmony and seek to get these expressed - because emotional stagnation upsets them more than anything. They can't abide lack of action on the water front, or lack of any real emotional connection between people. They'd rather people were yelling and expressing their dislike of each other than to have them pretending indifference to each other. Remember – Cancer wants to get the water energy flowing!

Scorpio: for deep, determined, secretive, loyal and possibly jealous characters

Scorpios are often described as being 'deep and impenetrable' sorts.

Their feeling nature is shrouded in secrecy and kept well-hidden and away from the surface. It is important to realise that it is *because* the feeling nature is so painfully intense that Scorpios need to cover it up so well. They are so good at it, in fact, that they can often appear impassive – you don't get the instant emotional reactions that you can with the other two water signs. They'll reserve their judgements for a little longer and you may never ever get to know how they're feeling about things. But make no mistake about it, your Scorpio character is not unmoved by matters, no matter how calm they may appear on the surface. They are profoundly sensitive and very much affected by the emotional undercurrents going on around them.

Thus, they may appear inscrutable themselves whilst doing the finest of jobs scrutinising everybody else. Despite the cool exterior there is often the sense that underneath 'still waters run deep', and they may be described as 'broody'. To 'brood' over something, according to the New Oxford Dictionary means to 'think deeply over something that makes one unhappy'. The feeling, the emotion which is being felt is being mulled over and chewed over slowly, as this is how its meaning can be assimilated.

'Fixed water' people hold onto the feelings for as long as possible before releasing them. It's a bit like the part in the middle of the book where all the issues which were introduced in the first part have to be mulled over and stirred gently around in the cauldron for a bit so they can 'cook' into whatever the resolution will be.

With all this water being stored under pressure there's a bit of a feeling of a pressure cooker about Scorpios at times. They might seem like they're about to explode at any minute. They are described as 'powerful' because of just that – the latent explosiveness, which if harnessed properly can be very powerful indeed.

Then there is the reputation that Scorpios have for being the sexiest sign of the zodiac. Or at the very least, the sign most interested in sex. Does this mean they will automatically make good hero material? It obviously depends on what kind of hero you want or need. If you bear in mind that the driving force behind Scorpio is water (emotion, in other words, passion) and that the 'type' of water is fixed (i.e. passion that has had a chance to build up, has not been dissipated but is held in place), you can see why they might be seen as exuding a restrained, pent-up sexuality. This is good if you are looking for a sensitive, strong, and silently yearning type. If, however, all that pent-up passion came out in an undirected and unrestrained way when it did finally show then you could be looking at someone with a cruel streak in their nature.

One of the key words to think about when creating Scorpio characters is 'power'. Power is important to them. It doesn't necessarily have to be overt, but they like to feel in control of the situation. For Scorpios, the stakes that they are interested in are always high ones. They aren't concerned with trivialities. If something matters to them, it matters very much.

Scorpio is ruled by the planet Pluto (otherwise known as Hades, god of the underworld) and by association is obviously associated with 'death'. And sometimes it can feel that all the things that are of importance to them are of 'life or death' significance. The 'life' part of the equation means that scorpionic people are often healers of various sorts. They could be actual physicians or therapists or just people who simply help to heal others in various capacities. The 'death' part means that they are agents who will effect profound and lasting change wherever they go.

As everything matters so much, clearly, this isn't going to be the type of character who jumps into bed with the hero/heroine and simply wants a 'one-night stand' or 'uncomplicated sex'. For Scorpios, sex will often be an almost sacred act and cannot be divorced from the emotion which they experience in connection with it.

This goes partially towards explaining why they may gain a reputation for being jealous types. Because of their extreme sensitivity, Scorpios are often very careful who they let into their highly-guarded emotional inner sanctum. Once they've let someone in, their anxiety around keeping control over things can become manifest in a desire not to let their mates stray too far. The emotional connectedness with their mate is something they hold very dear – and not something they will gladly share with others. Hence the reputation for possessiveness and even jealousy. It can be seen from this that the biggest fear that a Scorpio has is that of Betrayal. By the same token, one of the greatest gifts that a Scorpio can bestow is his loyalty.

Think of the king Aragorn in Tolkein's Lord of the Rings trilogy and you have an example of someone who is emotionally connected and yet who harnesses the power of that connection to achieve his aim. Whilst it is stated that 'Dwarves seek gold, Men seek power', Aragorn says quite clearly that he does not seek power, he fears corruption too much. He is aware of the dark side of his own nature, because Scorpios are 'broody' as we said, and they mull over what all those emotions inside them actually mean. In esoteric terms, the lesson that water signs are meant to learn is the Lesson of Peace.

Aragorn understands instinctively that peace can sometimes only be obtained through struggle; that it cannot be achieved by holing oneself up in some stronghold or fort (in this case Helm's Deep) and hoping that your enemies will wear themselves out before they wear you out first. Aragorn finally succeeds in achieving his own personal peace, (he fights the inner demons of the legacy of his disloyal and unworthy ancestors), and the crown of Gondor returns to him as the rightful heir, in the end.

Pisces – for compassionate, emotionally fluid and psychic characters

This is the stage of the water element that desires to change what *is* and move on to something else. Feelings are then experienced as being fluid and changeable. Moods race in and out. From the stalwart fixity of Scorpionic emotion, here the order of the day is to move on and change. Thus Pisceans may appear emotionally unsteady to those who like to know where they stand and who need things to be reliable and predictable. But within every system there is an inbuilt need for change and the water element is no different.

Pisces is ruled by Neptune, god of the oceans, and if there's one thing we know about the ocean it's that it can go from appearing supremely calm one day to being a heaving mass of unrest the very next day. And why should this be? There's something about the fact that the ocean is so vast, that makes its unpredictability in some sense acceptable. We accept that things may change dramatically through no obvious cause *because* the ocean is so large. In other word, the ocean is so big and uncharted that there may be unseen forces at work. There is more going on than can be seen 'on the surface' We accept this with the ocean, where tidal waves may materialise out of previously calm waters, because we know that 'what you see' is not always 'what you get'. What you see is just the tip of the iceberg. Many strange creatures live in the benthic depths of the ocean that we will never encounter in our lifetimes; we know this. The sea represents the huge untapped reservoir of the unknown; the greatest proportion of life on earth, that we still know nothing about.

In just the same way, Pisceans seem to be able to tap into the vast reservoir of all that is unknown in the human psyche. Like the sea, they can be calm one moment and appear very emotionally charged the next.

Daisy Buchanan, in Scott Fitzgerald's 'The Great Gatsby' is

one such fluid creature. She appears to be as emotionally fluid as one can get, giggling over nothing at all one minute, and then sobbing wholeheartedly over a simple thing like being shown Gatsby's shirts because they are 'so beautiful'. Although Daisy is a sympathetic character - she is described as beautiful, and is charming, in fact, captivating, to all who meet her - the narrator, Nick, describes feeling a certain unease at times around Daisy. Nick feels there is some kind of insincerity about her (he's picking up on her inconstancy of heart) and is uneasy when he feels that Daisy wants to exact some sort of 'contributory' emotion from him.

Nick's reaction reflects how uneasy we all get from time to time when we are dealing with matters we don't fully understand or have any real grasp on. This could refer to the depths of the human psychological condition, or it could refer to the ability of some humans to go way beyond what we really 'should' be able to know and to know much more. A lot of people feel uncomfortable around psychotherapists/psychologists because they feel their innermost secrets will be seen at a glance. Many people feel the same way about clairvoyants and psychics (and I'm referring to the genuine article here, not those who fraudulently set themselves up to be something they are not). The thing that links the Piscean character in with both of these examples is that – like the two fish which form the sign of Pisces – the Piscean is able to swim in the sea of the unknown, traversing uncharted waters. They are able to go to places that others cannot. Einstein was a Piscean – and a mystic at heart.

Pisceans are amongst the most intuitive of the signs. They will know what they feel about things, but will very often not be able to explain *why*. That doesn't mean they aren't right in their judgements just as often as those of us who can explain what we mean.

The famed compassion of Pisceans can also be understood in the context of their watery origin. If you think of the ocean as being the source and the origin of all life, the fact that the fish can swim in and out and amongst every part of it, goes some way to explaining how Pisceans can 'put themselves in others' places' with such ease. We can easily think of the ocean as being a self-contained eco-system. We understand that anything we do to the waters of the ocean will affect all the creatures that live in it. Likewise, Pisceans have a very strong sense of the connectedness of all things. They intuitively know that our separateness is nothing but an illusion. Little wonder then, that Piscean characters often seem to know so much more than they really 'should'. Like the ocean they are fluid. They are not held within the boundaries of their own individuality… they can reach out and feel what others can feel.

This type of character might also typically have an addictive nature. Like the ocean which is full of water which will not slake a thirst, they may continually 'thirst' for something which cannot be satisfied. This is because the things which people get 'addicted' to are only ever substitutes for what the soul really longs for. In the case of the Piscean, what is longed-for is a return to a state of eternal bliss; thus they make natural mystics, priests, empaths and addicts with equal facility.

As you can imagine, a character who very easily takes on the pain of others, might also need to find some way to escape from that pain. Escapist tendencies might also be evident. This can show up in a positive way – for example by way of a fantastic imagination, useful for writers! – Or, it may be channelled less positively and end up as a stubborn resistance to facing up to the realities of life. That way also leads us down the route of addiction. Thus Piscean characters may be our shamans or they may be society's dropouts.

PART TWO

EARTH

Earth – the element of groundedness
and the five senses

Earth people are the ones who are attuned to what we can see/ touch/taste/smell and hear with our physical senses. They are the ones who are the best 'grounded'. They are stable, steady as rocks, appearing solid and reliable. Unlike the other elements, earth does not appear to move very much. Its cardinal quality is that it does not move or change. We use earth as the yardstick by which we can judge progress; we use distance travelled upon the earth in miles and the amount of a thing can be measured in terms of its weight, its height or its breadth. We number the days we spend upon the earth in terms of the minutes and hours we can count on the clock. We measure our worldly success by how many things we can accrue while we are here.

If you were to go outside right now and pick up a handful of soil from the garden, then the contents of your palm would reveal straight away what the nature and function of people attuned to the earth element really is.

For starters, that handful of earth might contain bits and pieces of the roots of plants. The element of earth is responsible for rooting us and grounding us, just as the real earth holds in place the root structures of plants. We could say that Earth provides a rooting system and an anchorage point for the soul. That's what earth people do for us, too. They are the bedrock upon which everything else can stand. Basically, 'earth' tunes us in to what *is,* right at this moment. It follows that **the time frame that Earth relates to is the here and now.**

It is in the nature of *all* energy to flow. Earth is no exception to this rule. But the earthly flow of energy is in terms of, and connected to, earthly things. So, earthy people are interested in moving about things like, e.g., money (they become bankers and business men), organic matter (through agriculture and animal husbandry – they may become farmers or gardeners), and the moving of actual physical structures (so they may go in for building, construction work or even things like architecture or building planning).

The other thing you might find in that handful of soil is a batch of seeds. The earth is the archetypal mother. So, the earth-element expresses the essence of gestation in every form. As gestation is about waiting for something to come to fruition, earth people can be wonderfully patient and persevering. Basically, they have an innate and organic understanding about the cycles of time. They are willing to dig in deep and wait for the results which they intuitively understand will come in their right season.

Earthy people hold the seeds of what can be manifest and what can be brought into being. Whilst a water person might *long* for something, and an airy person might draw up *plans* for that thing and a fire person might very vividly *imagine* that thing, it is the earth person (or the earth element in each of us) that makes the thing actualise on the earth. They basically get things done. They understand how to go about life so as to make things actually happen.

The other things you might find in your handful of soil are; little rocks and pebbles and minerals which come from the surrounding bedrock and stones which may have been washed there by ancient rivers. These are the earth's 'treasures'. If the earth were an animate conscious being then we can imagine that a little sliver of quartz would be no less a treasure to her than a nugget of 'gold'.

As treasures – both in real and metaphorical terms are the domain of the earth, so it falls to earth people (and the earth element in each of us) to define, clarify and bring into consciousness *what is of value and – by extension –* what our values are. As we are talking about people who are very concerned with 'values' it follows that earth characters are going to have a high investment in what 'other people think'. They place a great deal of importance in laws, codes, standards, and 'how things appear in public'. They are going to move the earth energy about in highly structured and conformist ways (e.g. buildings must be built according to safety regulations and within the proscribed budget). They will insist that societies are run along such-and-such lines in accordance with the wishes of the 'founder' (importance placed on the roots). They will treat their forbearers (who again represent roots, where they've come from) with veneration and respect.

Our most venerable forbearer of all, mother earth, is also respected by those who, as farmers of the land, earn their living from her.

As you begin to get a sense of the earth element energy and the kind of personality that would be attuned to earth, you can also see how 'earthy' people might interact with the other elements.

Being steady and enduring, earthy people have a tolerance and affiliation for water people. Earth needs water in order for the soil to be productive instead of sterile. Water provides one obvious mechanism for movement of earth energy (and remember all energy wants to move!)

Both earth and water are Yin (passive, receptive, feminine) elements. They tend to be 'done to' rather than 'go out and do'. Take this in the broadest possible sense. Of course earth people and water people go out and do stuff, for themselves as well as for others. But we're talking about a basic orientation of energy here. And, looking at elements in nature this is borne out. We don't often see earth energy moving of its own accord (continental drift is so slow that it is unnoticeable for most of us and volcanic activity is rare) – it tends to *be moved* by air or by fire (which changes it), or sometimes carried away by the movement of water.

The other two elements, fire and air, have their own internal mechanisms for movement, so to speak. They are 'movers'. So it is with the characters that attune to these elements. They tend to be people who radiate energy outwards (as opposed to inwards); they are more extrovert whereas the first two are more introvert.

So; earth people deal with money and banking (treasures); they deal with the foundations (roots) of both our buildings and also the building blocks of our society and our institutions. In other words they deal with laws (lawyers, police, high court judges), and social mores. Let us now look at each of the earth signs in more detail.

Capricorn – characters for whom reputation, social standing and long-term ambitions are paramount

Capricorn expresses an earth energy which - while having all the earthly drives and values of the other two - still isn't afraid to open up possibilities and examine possible ways and means of achieving its purpose. When we talk about 'earth' we are talking about earthly, tangible things that can be seen and felt and heard and worked with, like tablets of clay or rules of law. Basically, this means things that in some way have a shape or a form or a boundary. The Capricorns will be the ones who sow the seeds of the business, write the laws, and lay down the format for whatever 'earthly' structure it is that follows.

Capricorns are often given the reputation of being 'ambitious'. Why this might be so, is understood in terms of what it is the energy of the first stage of earth sets out to achieve. Anyone who sows a seed has a vision of the way things might be in the future. They have a plan for what might be – even if they know it may take many years for that seed to germinate and come to fruition, they've got an idea in their head that it will happen, and that it *can* happen. Sowing a seed is an act of faith. Beginning any earthly project is an act of faith. But it isn't so much a spiritual act of faith as it is a soulful one. Earth signs understand that the rise and fall of earthly things – the growth of a seed or of an empire – have an inbuilt organic timing all of their own.

Just as the face of the earth we live on is subject to the changing seasons, earth signs accept that 'To everything there is a season'. They start their projects off knowing that fruition will come at the end of a – sometimes very long – wait. This is where the Capricorn capacity for patience comes in (and the attribution of longevity).

So, Capricorn is step one in the process of moving earth energy. As a character, Colleen McCullough's Ralph de Bricassart in The Thorn Birds is a prime example of someone motivated by ambition. Actually Ralph has two ambitions. More nobly, one of his ambitions is to become the 'perfect priest'. He wants to become a vessel so filled by God that he no longer desires worldly things. Yet he hankers after worldly power, too. He would look magnificent, the rich dowager Mary Carson tells him, in cardinal's red.

Mary understands that Ralph's ambitions pull him both ways simultaneously. Piqued by her unrequited love for him, she accuses him of being incapable of loving. Ralph *does* love a woman – Meggie Cleary, but he sacrifices every chance of human connection, all of his sensual nature, his maleness, his love of quality things and riches, in return for the prestige of becoming cardinal. Meggie bears him a son, who dies before Ralph ever knows that he has one. In the end, Ralph recriminates himself with the knowledge that he wanted the title of 'Cardinal' more than he wanted his own son. His heart is broken, but Ralph is not ruled by his heart. He is far too ambitious for that.

But maybe we shouldn't judge him for it. He makes his choices based on his prime directive which is an earthy one. He has to climb the ranks. It is the thing that matters most to him. Poor Ralph suffers later when he realises that becoming a church leader was only a substitute – an outer symbol – of the thing he originally wanted, which was 'to become the perfect priest'. He also realises the hubris implied in that desire; ultimately, he denies his need to be a father to his son, his need to love a woman, his earthly needs. He denies his own nature and so he suffers.

'To be ambitious' is something that is often frowned upon in our society. It might be something to do with the idea that we should all 'know our place' and keep to it. Even Mark Anthony, speaking about Caesar, comments that 'noble Brutus hath told your Caesar was ambitious; if it were so, it was a grievous fault'. Capricorns, though, are very aware of their 'place' – and everyone else's 'place' because they have a strict sense of social decorum and the natural order of things. This is why they are often prepared to wait a long time and to put a great deal of effort into their rise to the top. They don't want to be seen as upstarts but they want acknowledgement that they have got to their place through their own merits. They want rewards that are important in the world, and that will increase their standing in society. This is the primary motivation behind Capricorn energy.

Taurus – for patient, persevering, steadfast and sensual characters

Taurus next. This is the type of earth energy that doesn't want to change. It's in the middle. Its function is to keep things going exactly as they are.

If you want a prime example of what the pure and unadulterated energy of the Taurean can be like, pick a Hobbit, any Hobbit. In 'The Hobbit' the picture is very soon drawn of a quiet, unobtrusive little people who adore food and have hairy soles to their leathery feet. Apologies to any Taureans who may be reading this who do not have fat stomachs or sport any thick brown hair on the soles of their naturally leathery feet. But the rotundness and the preference for two dinners come from the natural love of good food. Earth people are sensualists above all else, and of course food evokes four of the senses at once – sight, taste, touch and smell. And those bare feet must make such good contact with the earth when they are walking about on it all day. The Hobbits are excellent gardeners.

Here we are talking about **fixed** earth, of course, so we would expect these characters to be conservative by nature. They don't like change. Moreover, the premium on social structures and sticking to the rules of the 'way things are done around here' will be high. So we learn on the very first page that the Hobbits known as the Bagginses had lived in the same location (the Hill) just about forever, and that people considered them very respectable (bound by social mores and dictates), not only because of their affluence (i.e. they had accrued physical and tangible evidence of their earthly wealth), but also because of their extreme predictability. In fact, you wouldn't even have to ask a Baggins what their opinion was on any given subject because you would already know exactly what they would say. And you can't really get much more conservative than that.

The Hobbits, we also see, are more inclined to duck quietly

out of trouble's way rather than confront anything head on. The way with fixed earth is to just stand steadily and quietly and firmly and hope that things will sort themselves out in the end. This can give the reputation for tending to be languid or laid back. Even indolent. But Taureans are not given to precipitous action or jumping in with both feet to try and change the way things are. They like everything exactly the way it is,

Bilbo Baggins reminds the wizard Gandalf of this, saying he doesn't want any adventures today thank you (remembering his manners even under the duress of someone trying to foist something as unrespectable as an adventure onto him).

Taurus is ruled by the planet Venus, sensual goddess of Love, and this ties in with the Taureans' earthy orientation towards the senses. The primary motivation for this type of character is never going to be too far from home or too difficult to work out. It will be right there, under your nose. What you see is what you get. Their goals will be easily definable ones. They won't have hidden agendas running alongside what they claim to be after. The first and primary motivation will be to secure comfort and safety. Safety for the body can be found in a strong and durable home filled with comfortable things. Later on, safety in a psychological sense may be gained from a feeling of belonging to something that has endured for a long time - a family name, a community, a belief system. They like the familiar, they like the tried-and-tested. They also like to feel that they are contributing something towards the established order, and that they are doing their part to help the old order endure.

Virgo – for characters who are discriminating, independent and desire to serve others

The final stage in earth energy relates to where the process is finished and ends are tied up so that life can move onto something else. The thrust of this energy is towards finishing off and changing. To put it another way, the drive here is to manifest something into the physical world that brings about a change in the earthly structures that currently exist.

When Vianne Rocher arrives in the little town of Lansquenet-sous-Tannes (*Chocolat,* Joanne Harris), she decides to stay, on the intuition that the place is in need of a little magic. Being earthy by nature, Vianne's magic is of an earthy, sensual sort. She opens the chocolate shop extraordinaire, a veritable feast for the senses just as the traditional season of denial, Lent, is about to begin. Vianne's action will have the effect of bringing great change to the institutions that exist in the village. Vianne knows this. She casts the tarot cards and up comes Death. This card represents Change, we are told. Something is about to upset the status quo.

This is Vianne's function in the story – to bring about that change and when it is done she will leave. She even tells her daughter at the beginning of the story, they will stay on 'until the wind changes'.

True to the archetypal energy of Virgo, Vianne is highly perceptive and discriminating – she can tell the subtle difference between a thousand different types of chocolate – and so she can measure change even when it occurs in infinitely small amounts. This finely-honed ability to discriminate between earthly things that we see in Virgo is linked to their primary function – which is simply to bring about that change.

It is this highly developed ability to discriminate that has led to the Virgo reputation for being 'perfectionists'. There they are, worrying about the tiny little details that nobody else even notices, we say, and *why?* The reason is because they *can* tell the difference!

They are like a macro lens focused right down on all the little things that go to make up the picture. Sometimes they are so focused on the minutiae that they can't see the big picture, that's true. But then, that isn't their function. Their raison d'etre is to hone in on what makes things different from each other. The Virgo purpose is to be able to tell what discriminates one thing from another – just as their opposite sign, Pisces, has the function of being able to tell what it is we all have in common and what makes us all the same.

This leads on naturally to the Virgo's own sense of self as being one of a very autonomous being. According to Liz Greene, the word 'virgo' originally meant 'intact' – or to put it another way, 'whole'. Virgos see themselves as being complete in themselves. This has sometimes given them an unfair reputation for being aloof. Yet the Virgo desire is to serve others, and very far from actually being aloof.

Another word that is sometimes used to describe Virgo is 'analytical'. This goes with their penchant for examining how things are different from each other. Virgos are good at classifying things. They can see how things can be put into different boxes and labelled in such a way that information can be retrieved according to a system of classification. Like Gemini, Virgo is ruled by the planet Mercury, god of information. But Geminis collect information for its own sake – just because they are interested. Virgos collect information because they want to put it in a particular classified order; they want to *do something useful with it.* This fulfils their primary motivation which is to be of service, using their ability to discriminate between worldly things.

PART THREE

FIRE

FIRE - the element of Inspiration and Imagination

What fire does in nature is, it burns up a substrate in order to create something else, namely, light and heat. So, we speak of 'fiery' people as being full of warmth and maybe hot-tempered and we can acknowledge their insights as being 'illuminating' and far reaching. It is in the nature of fire (as it is of air) to spread out towards the perimeter. We call them trailblazers.

Fiery people are at home in the world of the imagination, because that is the realm of fire. They help create the future by imagining what it will be. People are very much drawn to fiery characters, just as people are drawn to watch a candle or towards a lighted hearth in a darkened room.

What fire expresses is the power of creation – and fire people can be very self-conscious about and absorbed in this ability of theirs to create. It can be thought of as a gift from the gods, just as we know Prometheus had to steal fire from the gods in the first place, in order to give it for the betterment of mankind.

According to esoteric wisdom, the soul journey for fire signs is to **Learn how to Love**. If fire people are sometimes portrayed as being very much in love with themselves (think of brash Aries, showy Leo and dramatic Sagittarius), then it is because everyone has to learn how to love themselves first before they can love anyone else

With all the fire signs there is a need and a desire to draw others to them, in order to feed off their admiration. This is the substrate that the fiery character needs to feed off – by others' acknowledgement of them, fiery people come to appreciate and understand their own beauty.

The other cardinal quality of fire is its ability to illuminate things. This ability to 'shine the torch' means that fire people are often blessed with flashes of foresight – not to mention insight. They can look forward with a finger on the pulse of the trend that is about to develop. They make terrific entrepreneurs and style gurus because they can 'see' the future that is about to develop long before anyone else.

There is an ethereal, other-worldly quality to fire. Whilst it attracts us it might also burn us. Likewise, whilst people are attracted to fiery types there may also be an innate fear that such types won't really make such suitable long-term partners. Fire isn't at all steady. It wobbles about, sparks out and moves on just as soon as ever it can.

Enthusiasm

There is a touch of the larger than life 'super-hero' about fiery people; they have something of a reputation for wanting to rescue the weak and the meek and the damsels in distress (think Firemen!), or they may simply want to be champions of a cause but either way they've got to be champions and heroes to feel truly happy.

Fire people have a huge capacity to fantasize and mythologize (this goes with the 'larger than life' territory) - for fire people, the world of fantasy and myth IS the real world. This is why they make such good story-tellers and dream-weavers; they can spin out the best yarns of all. Just as fire is wobbly and without shape – the way fire people experience 'reality' needs to be likewise fluid and to retain its potential for movement. This is why many fire people like to move around a lot. They like to travel, and to explore. Both physically, visiting different locations on the earth, and mentally, they like to explore possibilities, so they become philosophers and priests and spiritual devotees who explore other realms.

Once a fire person latches onto an idea, they have the capacity to infect others with their own light – 'enthusiasm' comes from the Greek, 'en theos' meaning 'filled with god' – and everybody who sees that wants a little bit of it for themselves.

There is a joy and a freedom and a playfulness about fire that is very attractive. All the fire signs are children at heart.

They remind us of our own childhood – when everything was still possible and we still believed in the big stories and in magic and we had it all to play for. Of course, lovely though children are, they can be hard work. They don't want responsibilities. Fire people can have trouble in dealing with the mundane (boring!) real world and this includes dealings with their own body.

They can be impatient with people who don't have their insight and intuition, but who are responsible, slow and methodical and good at 'reality'. **The time frame which fire is linked to is the future.** Fire deals with the realm of what might be, what could be – so just as the light from a fire 'lightens' up a room and aids vision, so the same element can 'enlighten' fire people and give them 'vision'.

Let's now look at the three signs that make up the element of fire.

Aries – for characters who are fearless, action-orientated and jump head-first into things

As Aries begins the element of Fire, the whole thrust of an Aries character's meaning is to do with spreading fire out, or to put it another way, **inspiring** others **through** one's own **action.**

Just like the ram goes at things 'head first', Aries characters are also reputed to rush straight at things without always stopping to consider what the consequences might be. Basically they just get on with it. Whilst this may lead to many mistakes which they afterwards regret, it also leads to an experience-rich life. One thing they will not regret is that they lost too many opportunities along the way, missed out on too many experiences, because they were afraid to fail. Aries characters don't stop to worry about whether they will fail or not. They just *do* it, whatever it is. That in itself is often inspirational for others. They aren't afraid of getting hurt. They trust that they will survive. At the very least they trust that the part of them which matters most will survive.

Picture the scene in the film 'Gladiator' where Russell Crowe's character, the brave and battle-hardened Maximus stands in the arena facing the emperor Comodus, murderer of his wife and child. The whole film has been building up to this one scene. It is the one where Maximus gets to take his revenge on his mortal enemy. We have had many opportunities to witness Maximus' honour and integrity in action. We want to see the ruthless and sadistic Comodus get his come-uppance.

In this scene there is absolutely no question about "What's my motivation, Mr De Mille?" Maximus has got to take Comodus' life and there are no two ways about it. In achieving this against all odds, Maximus becomes, in the eyes of the crowd, a hero of almost mythological status. No other ending would have worked because Maximus is already the perfect embodiment of the element of fire. He is truly a hero, endowed with inspirational and leadership qualities. He has a vision for the future. He is a vanquisher. He is unafraid to create or destroy. He is more interested in *Action* than in thoughts or words. Fire is very capable of annihilation as we know.

This is exactly what Maximus does. He knows he will die, but his courage inspires those he leaves behind to seek the 'dream that once was Rome' – that of a Republican empire.

Maximus is a good example of the Aries principal on another count too, because Aries is ruled by Mars, god of War, and of course Maximus is a soldier and fighter above all else. Mars isn't just about war, though. He stands for the principle of 'taking action'. Our Aries characters will also always be people who are willing to 'take action' – both on their own behalf and on the behalf of others. They will not sit back to 'wait and see' how things develop. Sometimes they will jump in precipitously, feet-first, and get into a big mess. But no-one will ever doubt their motives or their courage.

The thing about being the first sign of the zodiac, is that Aries – being the leader – doesn't always stop to think about all the other characters that come behind him into the fray. That is, Aries characters can be self-centred. They can even be downright selfish. Part of that is because of the speed with which they typically act; they genuinely may not stop to consider other people in the equation before they take action.

Part of the deal with the planet Mars (which rules Aries) is that it is the planet which demands that we 'stand up and be counted'. There is no sitting on the fence and hedging your bets with Mars. You stick your head above the parapet for all to see and once you've done that there is no going back. People know where you stand. So from there on in you have to stand up for what you believe in. You can't just smile nicely and keep quiet about it, even if it means having a big argument with someone, you've got to do it. This is why Aries people are sometimes said to be argumentative. It is because it is their natural tendency to come out with what they believe in and stick up for it. You may not be willing to argue the toss, but you can count on it that they will.

Going all out to stand up for what you believe in may sometimes be admirable, and sometimes just be downright foolish. Discretion, as the saying goes, is the better part of valour.

Leo - for characters who are steady,
big-hearted and grand visionaries

This is the middle phase of fire where the energy does not wish to go anywhere. It simply wishes to give out heat and light and to show itself for what it is. Part of the steadiness of Leo characters comes from this 'knowing what and who they are'. There is often a sense of gravitas about them. They aren't trying to be anything else. They know that they are good enough, just as they are. You can think of it as a fire banked in a hearth. It isn't trying to go any where, it is just steadily being itself.

All the signs which are 'in the middle' have this ability to let the energy in question 'build up', and Leo is no exception. The Leo person is inclined to mull over his visions and dreams which can consequently grow very big and grandiose because they are not scattered everywhere but gathered together. If these dreams are then made manifest the rest of us can only gasp in amazement at the scale of the visions that are then unfurled before us in a glorious blaze of splendour. How can anyone even *imagine* all this, we ask (let alone bring it to fruition)?

The ruler of this sign is the Sun, which is apt, because it is the light and heat which comes from the Sun which allows life to exist on earth. Basically, this is the primary creative force. It is the heart and font of all that is created. Like the Sun, Leo characters like to shine. They *need* to shine, in fact. It is part of the purpose of their existence. Leos are sometimes credited with being 'showy' or 'show-offs' – but when you've created all this wonderful stuff what else would you want to do with it? It is said that Leos make good actors … (because acting gives Leo the chance to be on stage and to be 'on show') – but the true heart of Leo desires to show itself *for what it is*, and not as something else (as in pretending to be another character). If a Leo character does take to the stage, then their own persona as 'an actor' will have to be at least as important as any character part they play. Basically, they don't make the seamless kind of player who merges into the background and who gets to play many different parts without ever being recognised as 'themselves'.

Jay Gatsby, the mysterious self-made millionaire from Scott Fitzgerald's 'The Great Gatsby' is a good instance of this Leonine type of energy in fiction. We learn in chapter one that Gatsby's attention is fixed firmly on some kind of dream, some vision that he has for the future with the image that is given of Gatsby standing alone in the garden, stretching his hand out to a green light that is visible at the end of a far away pier. The green light becomes the symbol for the thing – the girl Daisy – that Gatsby's heart most desires. But despite Gatsby's fabulous wealth, we learn that his own family were poor and unsuccessful and that it is only through his incessant dreaming and scheming that Gatsby has made it, at all. Gatsby has created everything that he has and everything that he is – even his name is made up. Yet people flock to him, like moths to the flame. They are attracted to his fabulous wealth and his famed generosity. He is like the Sun shining in the midst of the solar system around which others can flourish.

Gatsby builds all his dreams upon the belief that he loves Daisy beyond all else, and that she feels the same about him. His quest for Daisy is likened to the quest for the Holy Grail – very apt for a fire character!

And as Gatsby so beautifully personifies Fire, it should have been Love that fuelled his meaning. But as Gatsby does not love himself, he cannot love Daisy. What he truly loves is the romantic illusion which surrounds Daisy because of her wealth. This is why Gatsby ultimately fails; it is because his fiery mission is flawed. He has not learned the lesson of Love.

And, very sadly, no one really loves Jay Gatsby either; when his fall comes, all his so-called 'friends' melt away into the crowd and don't even come to his funeral. This is what happens to would-be Leonine characters who express the 'outer show' of what it is to be a Leo but not the inner soul of it. A true Leo has a need to express their inner light (just like the Sun which rules Leo), but the person's station in life is not important. They don't need to be (like the lion is) a king; they just need to be in touch with their heart.

For Leo characters who *have* learned the lesson of love, there are few signs who can match the utter generosity of spirit of this one. This is because these Leos have learned that the sun will never run out of heat or light ... there is no need to stint on anything, because there is always more where that came from.

Sagittarius – characters who are explorers of the unknown, philosophers and visionaries

The focus here is to imagine things that have not been imagined before. Sagittarians are the explorers of the new. They constantly open up new pathways in the realms of the imaginable. A mutable fire character will therefore be one who will 'open up' your world and lead you on to previously unimagined things. When Hagrid the giant first reveals to the astonished Harry Potter - 'Harry – yer a wizard' - a magical moment of the opening up of Harry's imagination occurs. All sorts of things might now be able to happen that Harry – and the reader – couldn't have allowed before. It is as if mutable fire gives the person permission to dream hitherto undreamable dreams.

It isn't just about *imagining* what might be – it's about taking that imagination in a new direction. Fantasy stories, sci fi and all sorts of paranormal genre that conjure up totally new worlds, revel in this dimension of the fire element, where what is conjured up remains unfettered and new.

It can be seen why fire and air need to work so closely in conjunction – air fuels fire – and thought is often the pathway for new imaginative pathways to open up. It isn't always, though, because pictures and symbolic renditions can come without the need for the words which herald thought.

To put it another way, mutable fire describes a *vision* for a new world or a new way of being. The fire person can have the vision of what might be without having any idea of what structures need to be put into place in order to bring his dream into being. This is when he will need the help of an air ally. The air person (described below) will describe a new *system for thinking* or a new way of looking at things that will enable fire's possibilities to come into being. In other words, fire will dream it up and air will figure out how to make it work.

Jupiter is the planet that rules Sagittarius, and Jupiter is the planet of – above all things – *expansion*. One way this impacts on the Sagittarian character is that it creates a desire in this sign to always see the 'bigger picture'. These are the philosophers of the zodiac, the priests and the gurus, the teachers and the interminably curious who are willing to travel deep into the uncharted spaces of the world to 'find out' about things that have not yet been discovered. These are the people who always want to take a thing up to its highest level. They are absolutely not interested in the minutiae of life; they are not interested in the details. They want to know how everything dovetails in with everything else. They want the grand road-map of the universe, and they are willing to go further than anyone else to get it.

Being a mutable sign (the one which wants to 'end the process and move onto something else'), for Sagittarians, it is most definitely true that 'it is better to travel hopefully than to arrive'. They aren't actually all that interested in arriving. They just want to keep on travelling. They want to keep on learning (expanding their knowledge) forever; they want to keep on exploring the boundaries of the unknown. They make for exciting characters because there is a touch of the mysterious and dangerous about them; they are curious and they are unafraid, and often (being able to see the big picture so well) there is a touch of the sanguine about them. They can be philosophical in the face of life's problems. They can laugh and make light of things because they see that, 'in the grand scheme' their little worries are just that … little and insignificant.

Having said that, high-spirited visionaries who keep their sights on the grand goals and noblest of causes will often benefit greatly from having a well-grounded sidekick at home. This is where an earthy companion comes in handy – to make sure the socks get paired and there are groceries in the fridge for when the wanderer returns. Paired socks may be 'little and insignificant' in the grand scheme – but not all of life revolves around the grand scheme. Sometimes the little things *are* important and 'God is in the details'.

Nevertheless, the ability to explore their visions from all angles gives Sagittarians a keen entrepreneurial edge. The time-frame that fire relates to is the future, as we have already said – and so Sagittarians can 'see the road ahead' and are talented at predicting what is coming up next. Thus they make good businessmen, being able to predict trends ahead of time. No matter how successful they are, though, the ultimate goal is never just to make the money and to have the success and the accolades... the ultimate goal is to push the boundaries of what can be achieved further and further forward. It is, in fact, to imagine the impossible and then make it come into being.

PART FOUR

AIR

Air – the element of communication and mental relatedness

We generally only notice air because it moves. And the whole point of moving things around is that they get shared out and dispersed and other people get to know about them. So it is natural from this that Air is the element of communication (from the Latin communicare = to share). It is the element that binds us all together in the brotherhood of man.

Because air rises, we speak of people being 'in their heads' in the 'lofty realms' or in their 'ivory towers'. Nothing really pleases air people so much as a good debate or a new thought, or being able to make connections between ideas that hadn't been made before. And, having made their connections, they want to share them. Probably by talking about them or writing papers in journals or newspapers or somehow expressing their ideas. It is no coincidence that it is by way of manipulating the air in our throats that we can physically talk to each other.

It has been pointed out more than once that the air signs are the only signs of the zodiac without any animal symbolism; they are, basically, the most civilised (with all the good and bad that that entails!). Rationality is the domain of the civilised human. They are primarily reasonable.

The mediaevals used to call airy people sanguine. This refers to how they take things in good part, are capable of being philosophical and of reflecting on things so as not to get too emotionally involved. On the other hand this capacity for reflection can make air people seem cold at times, and it also limits their spontaneity. They will 'turn things around in their mind' before deciding what to do. They also like to consider others and the impact any decision will have on them. They like to try and work outcomes out before making their minds up and keep at all times 'open-minded' about things.

Airy people are also the ones who ask, more than any other

type, the question 'Why?'

We live in a world culture that has long encouraged the intellect and the development of the mind (e.g. Descartes; 'I think, therefore I am') – but this has sometimes been to the detriment of the intuitive and feeling functions. You can't explain away feelings, no matter how hard you try.

The gift of the air people is their ability to move outside of their own viewpoints/wants/needs and to be objective. Airy people can take themselves out of the equation when making decisions which gives them the reputation for being 'fair-minded' (Libra), high-minded (Aquarian) and quick-witted (Gemini).

When dealing with air people the key thing to be aware of is that they have to have a paradigm within which to operate. Thoughts all have to be pegged up onto a geometrical framework – almost like the way minerals will crystallise into a geometrical crystal structure. They cannot abide 'non-structuredness'. Not for them the chaos that watery and fiery people seem to thrive in; they need to find a pattern in things or else they flounder. It's as if Air is already wispy enough and insubstantial enough that without some form to cling onto it simply cannot exist.

Now we will take a closer look at the three Air signs.

Libra - for characters interested in harmonising, relating and understanding others' viewpoints

The lesson of the Air signs is the **Lesson of Brotherhood**. Libra starts the ball rolling in this regard because the thrust is to start moving the focus of mental (air) energy away from oneself and onto someone else. That is, Libra initiates relationships. Thus, Librans are assigned the symbol of the balance – as air begins to move outwards towards someone else, and other people's viewpoints are taken on board as well as one's own.

When so many – equally valid – viewpoints are being held simultaneously, it can be difficult to make up one's mind about things. Thus Librans are sometimes accused of 'sitting on the fence' and being unwilling to come down on one side or the other.

Librans are known as the peace-makers of the zodiac. They are the reconcilers; moving the focus of their thoughts from one end of the scale to the other is their raison d'etre. They desire to bring about a harmonious end to matters. And the way to do it is to expand one's thoughts to let in other possibilities.

When Romeo complains that he can think of nothing but Juliet, his friend Benvolio counsels him to forget her by doing just this;

'By giving Liberty to thine eyes; examine other beauties' – he argues for movement of Romeo's thoughts. Later on, again, he counsels –

'One fire burns out another's burning. One pain is lessen'd by another's anguish; one desperate grief cures with another's languish'. It is obvious that he is balancing 'one' against 'another' all the time. This leads Benvolio to have a more equable personality type too, for, as he observes to Mercurio,

'An I were so apt to quarrel as thou art, any man should buy the fee-simple of my life for an hour and a quarter' and Benvolio, being not so wrapped up in himself as the others are, is more aware of appropriateness of time and place simply because he remains at all times *aware of others*.

'We talk here in the public haunt of men' he reminds them, 'Either withdraw into some private place, or else reason coldly on your grievances, or else depart; here all eyes gaze on us.'

It is obvious that a good dollop of cardinal air energy (that is, the 'initiatory' bit of air) makes a character more sympathetic to the plights and thoughts of others and better 'balanced' and less egocentric than they might be. It can also give the archetypal Libran a 'laissez faire' attitude and a tendency to 'go with the flow' – making them popular as friends and companions because they don't put up too much resistance to others' ideas or suggestions. They are happy to go along with what other folk want.

Too much Libran energy can however, take them so far away from their own centre and their own ego that one may begin to feel they aren't really 'there' at all, in their own right, but exist only as observers in some way, of the action.

This is the case with the unnamed Mrs de Winter in Daphne du Maurier's 'Rebecca'. The poor girl seems to get pushed around like a pawn all over the place. All the really exciting action belongs to 'Rebecca' who is dead before Mrs de Winter ever arrives on the scene, and the latter's final fate is to spend the rest of her days in exile with the much older Max de Winter, who, we learn, murdered his first wife.

Of course not all Librans choose to use their capacity to see others' points of view in this way. They can use their skill to make excellent mediators for one thing; they can become the bridge between warring parties, using their balancing talents to bring differing points of view into harmony.

This role as a harmoniser ties in with Libra's ruling planet, which is Venus (like Taurus), who of course stands for harmony and peace in all relationships. Note that Libra does not *empathise* with the Other as much as understand where they are coming from. Libra is air, so it's a mental understanding, not an emotional one (which would be a water function). A Libran would not enter your emotional frame of reference as much as he would attempt to understand your way of thinking. The Libran is typically even-tempered because he does not want to engage his emotions as much as he wants to engage his thoughts; this is what it is most natural for him to do. It might be difficult to get him riled, therefore. It might be difficult to even get him to admit to feeling any emotion or any passion or desire for anything whatsoever. For a water person this might be a little hard to stomach, especially if they are the sort who needs a grand display of emotion in order to keep them happy.

Like all air signs, Librans are happiest when working within a fixed structure; they like a system with rules and order. They don't like chaos. Librans are said to make great dancers, probably for this reason. Dancing is movement with form and order. It is also movement which is made *in relation to someone else.* Libra is the first sign which truly understands that 'one' can be made more than just oneself by joining with another. The thrust of Libra is therefore to understand the 'Other' through acknowledging how he/she thinks, and encompassing their point of view.

Aquarius – for characters who are devoted to humanity and ideals, attracted to the esoteric and the strange, rebellious thinkers and revolutionaries

As a concept, 'Fixed Air' (the air bit in the middle which 'wants to stay where it is') can be a bit of a strange notion to get your head around because of course we mainly notice air that moves. When air doesn't move at all, e.g. during the electric moments when the atmosphere builds up before a storm, or when it's a hot sultry day and we complain there's 'not a breath of fresh air about', the feeling that an imminent or violent change in atmosphere is coming also goes along with it. When the air is too still we begin to long for a storm or a breeze or anything that will 'lift' the air.

Likewise, in a society where the thought process has been stultified, where people have been comfortably living in the same ways for far too long, there builds up an energy which longs for change. The thrust behind the energy of Aquarius is towards just this; the breaking of the storm, the 'lightening' of the heavy atmosphere; but the price which must often be paid first is that of a storm. Changing the way society thinks is often only achieved at a price.

If the element of air represents our thoughts and our ways of thinking and means of communication, then the Aquarians are known to be the 'rebellious thinkers' of the zodiac; they are the ones who will 'break away' most easily from traditional thought-patterns. They are on the edge of what is considered 'acceptable thought' trying out new ideas and new concepts, working always just on the edge of the paradigm, working towards the point where the storm, metaphorically speaking, will break. The 'Fixedness' of this element comes from two things; first it is the build-up of mental atmosphere just described, and secondly it is the propensity of this sign, having once achieved the 'breaking of the mental storm' to become quite fixed and rigid in adhering to the 'new' ways of thought. Having once changed things, Aquarian energy can be quite fiercely antagonistic towards anyone who then comes along and wants to change things again!

Air signs – and especially Aquarians - are often credited with making the best friends, amongst the zodiac. And Aquarians are renowned for being great lovers of humanity. Humanity, of course, is a notional concept that is greater (in airy minds) than any one particular individual. The 'greater good of the group' will often be at the forefront of their minds when conducting all dealings. They make great team players. When all is reduced to the most objective and de-personalised level, however, the potential for humour (or dangerous fanaticism!) is high.

The famed objectivity of the Air signs also depends on Air's ability to move. Air that can waft into every nook and cranny and go up and down and around corners symbolises the mind that can see many different points of view. Fixed Air can't do this. It is stuck. So it follows that Aquarians can very rapidly lose their objectivity and get stuck in a particular way of thinking.

In 'Mr Wroe's Virgins' (by Jane Rogers), God tells the prophet Wroe to comfort himself with seven virgins, and the congregation offer him their daughters. The story is a fictional account of what happens between the (historical figure) Wroe, and his new household, told from the point of view of the 'virgins'. Whilst the whole theme itself (of a church which is set up to run along separate lines from the established Anglican church) is Aquarian in nature, the views of Joanna, the most 'proper' and 'seemly' of all the virgins is a telling one. Joanna's initial reaction on hearing that the seven are to be chosen is one of delight. She believes that this heralds the dawn of a new era – that the promised part for the women in the new order has been remembered.

So far so good, this is breaking new ground. Joanna is welcoming the new, more inclusive way of thinking. She rejoices in it. But now the fixed air lack of objectivity comes into play. Whilst the other females in the church are horrified at the thought of being 'offered up' for service to the hunchback Wroe, Joanna assumes everyone must feel as she does and interprets their reactions according to her own frame of reference.

When some of them faint and cry out, on being chosen, she

assumes this is because of their joy. But most of them are far from sharing Joanna's sentiments. So much so, in fact, that one of them subsequently throws herself in front of a carriage rather than submit to going with Wroe!

Joanna is an extreme example of someone who is so far 'in their heads' as to seem completely blind to all the emotional and physical ramifications of the orders she is preparing to carry out, beyond their 'spiritual purpose' which is the only one evident to her. Later on, the women are required to carry out rather intimate 'punishment' techniques on men within the church who have sinned. When one of the other virgins remonstrates that such 'contact' might be construed as 'unseemly' Joanna is adamant that the women are only there as symbols, in order to carry out the chastisement. Joanna's logic is as faultless as a child's of course, and about as sophisticated. She seems to be deliberately ignoring that any other factors other than her own reasoning might come into play. Joanna is a good example of the air element at its most fanatic. Her thoughts – her beliefs – are so strong that she frames *everything* according to her beliefs, even when to do so flies in the face of all evidence to the contrary.

Gemini - for characters who are quick-witted, curious, interested in words and communication, concepts and variety

This is the stage of the air element where what has been achieved is rounded up so that matters can move on to something else. Air – for which read information, communication and mental activity – moves freely in this type of psyche. Mutable air people (Geminis) wish to pick up as much information as possible – they are habitual fact gatherers, interminably curious – and to spread it as far as possible. The means of dissemination of this information may be through speech or writing or any other effective communicative method.

It follows that people attuned to this format of the air element will make good writers, lecturers, teachers etc.

Geminis have got the reputation of being fickle; they are said to change their minds a lot (by which is meant, they change the way they are thinking). This follows on from the penchant Geminis have for collecting information; if you're thinking a certain way and then new contradictory facts come in then it follows you will probably need to change your thinking in order to take on board the new pieces of information. Their opinions change in order to reflect new incoming data. This makes them seem inconstant to others who do not bother checking the facts so often, or who wait a little longer before throwing in their lot with one faction or another. They aren't really inconstant; they are simply taking on board the new and incorporating it into what they know.

In Barbara Erskine's 'Lady of Hay', the heroine Jo Clifford is a hard-bitten journalist when we meet her, who 'learns fast'. She also prides herself on her objectivity. She is objective enough to be willing to try a 'past life regression' session with a hypnotist herself before embarking on an article in which she plans to debunk all the theories about reincarnation. The hypnotist who regresses her says that all he will need is an open mind. And he gets one; he says she is the best subject he has ever worked with.

As Jo lets in more and more information from her 'previous incarnation', the whole way she *thinks* about the people and the issues in her life begin to change dramatically. It is also typical for a mutable air person, that when she has come to the end of learning what she needed to learn about her 'former life', Jo chooses the airy (intellectual) method of writing it all down in a book so she can get it out of her system once and for all.

The sign of Gemini the Twins is ruled by the planet Mercury. Mercury as we know, was the messenger of the gods. He not only carried messages between the gods but he also carried them from the gods down to humans. In other words, he was an emissary from the divine realms. And so it would some times appear to be the case with Geminis. They can be truly inspired in the realm of words and concepts – thus making excellent wordsmiths, authors, comedians (word-play) and (the other side of Mercury, the Trickster), fraudsters too, because words can be used to beguile and confuse as well as to tell the truth. Thus Geminis make the best spin-doctors of the zodiac.

Mercury was a playful god – and Geminis are often credited with being playful and staying forever young at heart (and certainly mentally alert). There is a certain playfulness to much of Mercury's trickery – he does it for fun, and because people are so easy to dupe. Likewise with Geminis, there is often no immorality associated with any trickery they propagate – more of an amorality. They do it because they can. Right or Wrong – for them – does not come into it. This is not to say that all Geminis are amoral – it just means that the pure and unadulterated energy of Gemini does not concern itself with such things. It is mainly concerned with what potential for play there is in the matter at hand.

And Geminis are also said to be flirtatious… for the same reason. Flirting is fun. There really isn't any more to it, as far as they are concerned. Moreover, they *like* people, because people provide an endless variety of interesting differences. The interest and fascination that other folk hold for them is primarily on the intellectual level. They are said to be the 'social butterflies' of the zodiac, and are often unfairly described as 'inconstant' of heart.

It is not their hearts which are inconstant though – it is their thoughts, and for the reason that has already been explained above. Whilst it might seem infuriating to those who are more 'fixed' in their views about things, the Gemini propensity to 'change their minds' (mutable air sign) is really a great gift. If we cannot change the way we think about things, ultimately we cannot change anything at all.

'What's my motivation, Mr De Mille?'

Let us consider for a moment what different people can do with a big theme like Revenge. Whilst revenge is still revenge whichever way you look at it, the *actual outcome* of that revenge will depend on what is the thing powering the person who is seeking it. A fire person (like Maximus from the film 'Gladiator') will settle for nothing less than the death or annihilation of their antagonist. These are the people who have to make the biggest, most dramatic statements of all; even if it means their own demise (a fire left to rage unattended may eventually burn itself out).

A water person will want to see their enemy hurt on a deep *emotional* level. A mortal wound to the heart will do nicely – the person's actual death will not be required (in fact, the watery revenge-seeker will want the person to stay alive for as long as possible, suffering their emotional torment).

Contrast Maximus's revenge with the way Meggie behaves in 'The Thorn Birds'. Watery people's whole raisons d'etre are their connections of the heart. Feelings take precedence over everything else. From the moment the little girl Meggie meets the priest Ralph de Bricassart, there is an instant heart-to-heart connection between them that will last a lifetime. They love one another deeply.

But Meggie is the instinctual one, the water person in the equation. She is the one with the loving and trusting nature, the nurturer, and the natural mother. She clings to the belief that someday Ralph will make space for her in his non-secular life as a priest whereas he knows that he never will.

As Meggie hardens over time, coming to understand Ralph's betrayal of her (he chooses the power that belonging to the church bestows upon him over the warmth of Meggie's loving arms), she exacts the one revenge which can truly hurt the man she has spent a lifetime loving – and it is an emotional one. Instinctually, Meggie understands that the man inside of the cold cardinal has only one regret – that he has no heir of his own body, no legacy to follow him – a regret made more poignant by his attachment to a young priest who reminds him of all the things he once was, and what he could have been. Meggie only reveals that the young man is in fact Ralph's own son, *after* the youth has tragically drowned. She denies Ralph the emotional attachment he could have had to his son by withholding the information till it's too late. A cruel revenge indeed, coming from the broken heart of a woman spurned and very fitting too, as the water person will seek to take revenge by cutting their enemy off from the thing which is the most precious to water – emotional attachment.

An earthy person, on the other hand, wouldn't get involved in emotional shenanigans or get too steamed up with a pressing need to kill the offending protagonist. The earth person understands the power of *things*. Things that money can buy, and the power that worldly goods can bestow on anyone who has them. They might seek to bring their enemy from riches to rags, and drag their good name (social status) through the dust while they're about it. This is precisely what the heroine Beatrice does, time and again in Philippa Gregory's novel 'Wideacre'. Beatrice is a sensualist extraordinaire. She is a prime example of an 'earthy' person. Every move she makes from the beginning of the story is designed to bring her closer to owning the land belonging to her family, known as 'Wideacre'. She also has strong sexual appetites which she does not trouble to curb even when these are incestuous ones. She has no compunction about killing, first her father, then her lover, when these appear to be about to get between her and her goal. Owning the land is her primary motivator, not revenge, but when her husband seems to be about to get in her way (discovering what a truly horrendous character she really is), Beatrice takes her revenge on him for standing in her way. She sets about having him committed for insanity, has him accused of malpractice so that his doctor's license is revoked and manages (through power of attorney) to get hold of his entire inheritance, divesting him of his legacy, his name and his livelihood all at once. Beatrice's sting is indeed sharp. And her tools for stopping those who get in her way are all earthy ones (divest them of their money, their name, and their power/credibility).

An airy person will want to exact an intellectual revenge – perhaps by proving their moral superiority or by mentally outwitting their opponent. The 1974 winner of seven Academy awards 'The Sting' starring Robert Redford deals with just such an airy revenge. Redford plays a small time crook whose friend has been murdered by a vicious gang leader. Redford's character enlists the help of another con-artist who has fallen on hard times and they both set out to get even on the gang leader by pulling off a big con on *him*. They don't set out to kill him or to mortally wound his feelings. The revenge is designed to hurt him where it will hurt him the most. It will get at his pride in what he considers his area of most prowess – his ability to con others. On the surface, the revenge is enacted by relieving this guy of a lot of money. On the deeper level, he has been relieved of his 'airy superiority' – he has shown up to be less 'clever' (less capable of outwitting his opponents) – a fitting revenge against him, indeed.

Finally...

The key areas of interest for all the elements are summarised below;

Water characters will be most interested in matters of the heart. They will relate most easily to the past. The key lesson that the watery soul is here to learn is that of **Peace.**

Earth characters will be most interested in the mundane world and what they can actually sense in front of them. They are most interested in the here and now. The earthy soul is here to learn about S**ervice.**

Air characters are most interested in mental matters, pure thought, concepts and patterns. Their interest spans all time frames. The airy soul needs to learn the lesson of **Brotherhood**.

Fire characters will be most interested in their dreams and visions for what might be. They create and are most interested in, the future above all else.

The fiery soul is here to learn the key lesson of **Love.**

Perhaps one of the most interesting things to note out of all this is that **people can do the same things for different reasons.** Any number of people might be moved to join together in a common cause ('Ban the bomb', 'bring back marmite flavoured crisps'… it could be anything) – but they'll all have their diverse reasons for doing so. They might all support the same cause, but their reasons will be their own, and not necessarily shared.

Most of us take it for granted that our fictional characters are going to 'go on a journey' in our story, one from which they will emerge 'changed'. If our characters don't change or they haven't learned anything about themselves (apart perhaps, from in comedy) – then there seems to be precious little point to the story. In this 'Art imitates Life'.

If you think about it, though, the most believable characters never really *change*, as such. They just come to be more truly what they really were, all along; they 'discover themselves' along the way. It's as if they 'wake up' and remember their nobler purpose, in some way. Some might remember it too late. Think of the shocking scene at the end of the film 'Thelma and Louise' where the heroines come to a stark realisation about the way the whole of their lives have been led so far. They make a final bid for freedom – albeit at a terrible price – but it is a bid which affirms what they have always known (and repressed) all along, which is that they were born to be free. They were never *meant* to be in thrall to anyone else.

Some stories have happy endings, some don't. But just like in real life, even when the stories have a sad ending, it doesn't mean that our characters have failed. There is only one way to fail, and that has nothing to do with what our character may or may not achieve in the course of the story (or in a lifetime).

It has only to do with whether or not they remember what they were really about, all along.

Further reading

All Around the Zodiac, Bil Tierney (Llewellyn publications, 2001).

Astrology for Lovers, Liz Greene (Thorsons, Harper Collins 1989).

Astrology, Psychology and the Four Elements, Stephen Arroyo (CRCS publications, 1978).

Down to Earth Astrology, Stephanie Michaels (Angus and Robertson publications, 1988).

Relating, Liz Greene (Aquarius/Thorsons, 1990).

Bibliography

Chocolat, Joanne Harris (Black Swan).

Harry Potter and the Philosopher's Stone, J.K. Rowling (Bloomsbury).

Mr Wroe's Virgins, Jane Rogers (Faber and Faber Ltd).

Rebecca, Daphne du Maurier (Doubleday).

The Great Gatsby, F.Scott Fitzgerald (Penguin Classics).

The Hobbit, J.R.R Tolkein (Harper Collins).

The Lady of Hay, Barbara Erskine (Sphere Books Ltd).

The Return of the King, J.R.R. Tolkein (Harper Collins).

The Thorn Birds, Colleen McCullough (Gramercy Books, N.Y.).

Wideacre, Philippa Gregory (Harper Collins).